Average Genius -
A Political Guide for the Apolitical

By Dan Dressel

November 2010

This book is dedicated to my loving wife Amy for listening to my rants, clearing up my thoughts, and dealing with all the nights on the road I spent writing this.

A special thanks to all the people I've never met who inspired me to write this book; some living, some dead, some quoted, and all brilliant minds I can only hope to one day emulate.

My Boat to Damascus

The ferry ride from New London to Orient Point lasts a little under an hour. Sitting in the lounge, I lost cell service after 20 minutes, and since this was an unplanned respite from the grind, I decided to take the opportunity to enjoy the view.

The sun was out, the seas calm, and the light blue sky contrasted well with the deep blue Long Island Sound. It was a chilly but otherwise gorgeous day, and if I hadn't left my jacket in the car, I would have been out on the decking sucking in the salt air and feeling for a moment like it was I who was in control, taming the seas and moving the world forward!

But I wasn't outside, I wasn't in control, and the only thing tame was me - a lounge passenger entrusting my life to a group of people I have never met, as did every other person on this and many other boats, every day.

I began to relate how similar this situation was to the rest of my life. How I went about and did my work on the road, on the computer, around the house, putting my life and assets in the hands of thousands of other people, from fellow drivers to food handlers to IT professionals and today a ferry boat crew.

A lot of people are out there could conceivably make or break my life on a daily basis, and though none of them has any specific control, the potential to affect me is undeniable.

Yet the situation didn't cause me or, it would seem, my fellow passengers any concern. The guy in the booth next to me was asleep, the woman across the lounge reading a book, and other people around the boat were snacking on the pre-made sandwiches, laughing, soaking up the sun, and in general completely relaxed and happy. Calm seemed to be the order of the day.

Our collective moment of Zen is actually rather easy to explain because this boat and crew have been making the journey for a very, very long time.

Good weather or bad, these people take off from one side of the Sound and head over to the other multiple times a day. They are experienced, licensed, and are continually checking and re-checking their ship to make sure that everything works.

This is what they do, and they do it well.

They don't try and tell me, the passenger, how to sell my company's product. They don't tell the woman what she should read, the man how he should get more sleep at night, or the people up top how they should change their diet. They drive the boat, we do our thing, and everyone leaves safe and happy from the entire enterprise.

Now compare that to the current state of our national, state, and local governance.

The leaders in government, like the boat captain and his mates, have asked for the privilege of leading the nation. The citizens, like the passengers of the boat, have a lot of things on their plate to deal with, and largely leave the details of governing to our elected representatives.

Yet rather than let the citizens deal with their problems and staying focused on keeping the ship of state from crashing into the rocks, our leaders spend a whole lot of time, energy, and our money fighting over how best to deal with the problems of the citizens daily lives.

It's a sad state of affairs, especially because I wouldn't trust most of the people in elected office to be my bus driver, much less run my life.

Not that the people in government are stupid. They tend to go to the best schools, have a lot of ambition, and work very hard to reach a position of power. But they aren't trained to be my life coach.

Our legislatures at all levels are primarily trained as lawyers. A legislature full of lawyers is well suited for arguing about the law, finding ways to manipulate codes and statutes, and saying very little with a lot of words.

They are also uniquely qualified to find ways around the restrictions created in our Constitution - a document specifically designed to limit the power of our Federal government and it's power over the individual.

Over the last few decades, this revolving group of ambitious lawyers have used that talent to create a vampire class of bureaucrats, special interests, and dependents that provide votes for their benefactors and increase their power.

Through new agencies, departments, and commissions they now can decide for us, the free citizens of these United States, what our children should learn, what we should eat, whose habits and needs we should pay for, and how much of our money they will take before we even get handed a paycheck. In sum, they are taking an ever increasing role in what we do day in, day out.

Even if the advice and suggestions are good - which has happened - the use of tax dollars to repeat the advice good parents should give to their children hasn't actually made anyone healthier, happier, or improved anything. In many cases the intervention has made things worse.

Instead, the money that has been taken from the citizens to pay for these initiatives has succeeded in creating a larger government and buying the votes of government workers, unions, and recipients of entitlements.

Recent estimates show that fully 16% of the national income is used specifically on programs to buy votes - social welfare, corporate welfare, and directed subsidies. That doesn't include the cost of administering those programs - those are just the giveaways.

In the process of spending that money, our leaders have taken their focus off of the tasks that the government is uniquely qualified for and bound to provide to it's citizens.   It is a backward, dangerous, corrupt system that is - to steal a concept we hear from activists and politicians - completely unsustainable.

There is a better way.

A way that makes people happier and healthier, the nation stronger and in a better position to make the world safer, and uses the talents and potential of our best and brightest in a way that doesn't involve figuring out ways to take our money for the sake of increasing someone else's power.

The way has been called many things, but I like to call it the way of the Average Genius.

The principle revolves around the idea that 300+ million individual will make better decisions, come to better conclusions and solve far more problems more effectively.

While I am quite proud of the name I've chosen for this book and - and appreciate people not only adopting it, but also buying a copy of this book for all their friends, family, neighbors, and co-workers - I do want to point out the ideas are not, in and of themselves, actually new.

Adam Smith referred to the 'invisible hand of the market' in his book, Wealth of Nations. Calvin Coolidge and Ronald Reagan - both Presidents who oversaw amazing growth during their tenure - spoke about the need to keep government small and out of the way of the individual.

Dennis Prager, conservative radio host, portrays this principle from another perspective, and often says 'the bigger the government, the smaller the citizen'. Thomas Sowell, a Stanford economist, has written multiple books on the widespread problems increasing government causes in people's lives.

I don't have the background to deconstruct all of their theories, or the prestige to try my hand at creating a whole new way to argue the 'guns or butter' question, so I'll be quoting more brilliant and educated minds where it relates.

What I can speak to are my own experiences, some relevant data, and reasons why individuals and private groups do things better - no government necessary.

I am going to go through some real life scenarios I've experienced and what others have taught me, explaining where the G-Men need to get the hell out of our lives and where we need them to focus their attention.

As luck would have it, I'm writing this just after a moment in history where we can see exactly what disasters unfold when Washington takes on a wide variety of responsibilities for itself and finds itself unable to deal with problems that require government attention.

Watching the Deepwater Horizon rig explosion, the Coast Guard mistakes that caused the rig to sink*, and subsequent oil spewing into the Gulf of Mexico has been a real lesson in how bassackward our entire government has become.

A major ecological disaster was unfolding, and we witnessed a combination of union protection laws, environmental regulations, boom coupling compliance standards, and an Administration focused on enacting a 'fundamental change' in the relationship between the nation and the individual all standing in the way of quickly stopping the leak and keeping the oil from washing up on the shore.

The only thing the White House and the federal government managed to do is force BP, the company that leased the doomed rig, to put their it's assets into an escrow account to pay for the economic damage... while the oil continued to gush.

As many noted at the time, the President managed to change the focus to the one thing we all knew they could do well - figure our how to take someone else's money and redistribute it to others.

The fact that we already had a working system in place to decide liability in a disaster such as this - the courts - only serves to highlight where the real focus of today's leaders lie.

Instead of using the institutions and powers in place, they used the crisis to build their power and create new, more expansive, less accountable ways to take from one and give to another.

Of course, a government of lawyers, professors, and activists will continue to be unprepared to deal with crisis that demand their attention when all they excel at is arguing, posturing, finding scapegoats, and directing a wide variety of our resources toward their needs, not those of the individual citizens.

It is a history of misused power that makes it necessary for us all to work to take the power out of the hands of politicians, bureaucrats, lobbyists, and lawyers and put it back in the hands of the people who were entrusted that power by our founders, the people who made this nation great.

Which leaves it up to us. We need to find a way to get power back in the hands of the Average Genius.

*Hot Air, 7/30/10, Did the Government cause the Gulf spill? (http://hotair.com/archives/2010/07/30/did-the-government-cause-the-gulf-spill/)

The World as Viewed by a Hammer

I'd like to run briefly through the underlying reason why I have so little trust in politicians and the vampire bureaucracies they create.

As I've become more aware of the world of politics, looked back upon the history of this nation, and read the thoughts of great men and women in their memoirs, there is one unifying theme in the lives of powerful people, be they sinners or saints : winning and power trump everything else.

John McCain, reflecting on the campaign to become the GOP presidential nominee in 2000 and the South Carolina flag controversy, said it best:

"... it could come down to lying or losing. I chose lying."*

McCain openly says that winning is more important to him than honesty and his convictions.   This from a man whose entire public life has been based on the image of the honorable warrior, the man of integrity.

What does that say for those who don't have that legacy to live up to?

The cold hard truth is that politicians, activists, and even pundits are primarily interested in two things - winning office and increasing power for themselves and their party.   Everything they do revolves around those two goals.

To these people - whose fundraising, legislation, regulation, and victory depend on upon us all being outraged in their favor - the voters are nothing but tools to be used while necessary and placated between elections.

McCain proved this point by completely reversing his famed 'amnesty first, enforcement later' 2005 position on immigration and the border fence in order to fend off a primary challenge in

2010. Values and positions are flexible when elections are on the line.

This is one of many examples why we should view all politicians and partisans with a jaundiced eye. It's the perspective we will need to reign in the Ruling Class and get government back to the business of protecting our rights.

There are other reasons to keep close watch on those who have asked for the privilege to lead, one in particular that needs little explanation.

Tom Perriello, Democrat congressman from Virginia, put it so bluntly I'll defer to his comment during a summer 2010 town hall meeting:

> "If there's one thing I've learned up here (in Washington) and I didn't really need to come up here to learn it, is the only way to get Congress to balance the budget is to give them no choice, and the only way to keep them out of the cookie jar is to give them no choice, which is why – whether it's balanced budget acts or pay as you go legislation or any of that – is the only thing. **If you don't tie our hands, we will keep stealing.** "***

The fact is, we have created this type of leadership through inattention, greed, and subservience.

We asked for more services, more benefits, more perks, more entitlements. We've allowed ourselves to become tools in exchange for a handout, a contract, and assurance that what our best and brightest offered wasn't another way, but the only way.

We can only free ourselves from their clutches when we free ourselves from all the 'benefits' we've sold ourselves for since the Great Depression, and accept that we cannot outsource responsibility for our retirement, healthcare, and job security to a disconnected and incompetent group of politicians, bureaucrats, and hanger-ons.

With that in mind, laying out plans to remove ourselves from their toolbox will require sticking to some pretty strong principles, enduring some sacrifice - some of it ours, and some of it others - and fighting back against the howling of a lot of people who have come to depend on their status as tools-at-the-ready for whomever promises to pay for the privilege of using them.

That means finding, supporting, and promoting candidates that pledge to refrain from not only earmarks and out of control spending, but who will begin the painful process of stopping corporate welfare and subsidies for favored industries.

We need these politicians to end special tax breaks and regulations based on lobbying might; stop funding 'studies' and research initiatives paid for by the taxpayer and benefiting the best connected consultants and their governing allies; and propose and push for stopping the two tiered society corrupt government breeds - one tier for the politically connected, and another to pay their bills.

We have to elect leaders who are serious and committed to dismantling public sector unions, cutting back and closing the alphabet soup of commissions, departments, bureaus, and councils our federal, state and local tax dollars fund, and finding ways to cull the government herd.

These leaders need to be focused on simplifying the tax codes, establishing a standard by which laws are written so that even the least educated among us knows what they mean, driving the power back down to the individual.

First and foremost, our leaders need to be dead serious about ending the means, the apparatus, and the appearance of corruption.

I've got a great idea on how to kick off the process.

We need to establish a trustworthy government, and the best way to do that is to have public verification - annually - that our leaders and all governments minions are on the up and up. We need to have annual audits of everyone who receives direct government payments for any reason.

Every government employee, every politician, every corporation (as well as their executive officers and board members) - every recipient of taxpayer money needs to be subject to an annual accounting of their assets, income, and resources, and it needs to be done by the IRS.

It will be expensive and time consuming, of course, but it would be worth it to ensure that everyone who is being trusted with the power, privilege, and paycheck that comes with government affiliation is worthy of that position.

I'm not talking about filling out a form declaring income like they do in Congress. Randy 'Duke' Cunningham, Charlie Rangel, and William Jefferson all got away with graft and corruption for years before getting caught, and then only because they were either stupid, arrogant, or a mix of the two.

No, the forms and professional courtesy won't do. We need a full frontal audit complete with receipts, accountants, sweating assistants and frantic whispers in the hallway.

If nothing else, this will do a lot to keep people with more ambition than integrity from seeking office, and if done right these audits will combat the type of small time graft that infects zoning boards, city councils, police precincts, congressional offices, mayoral offices - anyone trusted with government power needs to justify their position by verifying that they aren't cheating the system they have asked for the privilege to serve.

Annually. Did I mention the part about spouses? I didn't?

Well, just to make sure that point isn't missed, we need public audits for all those working for-or-in an elected position, as well as their spouses.

I recommend that last part because we've recently learned it's just a little too tempting to pass half a million dollars in campaign cash to your wife when you hire her as a fundraiser. Isn't that right, Congressman Filner (D-CA).***

Once that's in place, drive the point home by introducing mandatory minimum sentencing that is twice the private citizen standard for anyone who commits a crime while in a position of public trust. For any offense.

Sandy Berger doesn't walk with a $50K fine, he spends 20 long years Leavenworth. Scooter Libby doesn't get a $250K fine, he pays $500K and actually goes to jail. No matter the crime, the betrayal of public trust demands a higher penalty.

Take advantage of your position and you get the paddle, not the ruler. Tar and feathers would be nice too, but the greens would probably protest, so we'll put that on the back burner.

That seems a hell of a lot more fair than a system where the average citizen loses their assets and freedom for defying the almighty tax laws, while the well-connected insiders who cheat on their taxes are put in charge of the Treasury Department.

Or a system where private citizens get busted for insider trading, but members of Congress and their staff just get rich.****

It may seem like I'm being a bit harsh, draconian, vindictive, and unrealistic with this prescription, especially since it would require a vote by exactly those people who would be most affected by the new standard.

Then again, some young blood Congressman or President-aspiring Senator/Governor would get a lot of attention and support if he/she were to push - vocally - for a change in the way government holds itself accountable.

It would also be amazingly informative to see how those currently in leadership react to the proposal.

With that information, the citizenry could send a powerful message for a cleaner government, and make sure leaders opposed to a less corrupt, more accountable government are given their pink slips the next time their seat comes up for election.

*Huffington Post, 8/6/10, JD Hayworth Campaign Ad Quotes John McCain Lying about Confederate Flag in 2002 (http://www.huffingtonpost.com/2010/08/06/jd-hayworth-campaign-ad-q_n_673142.html)

**The Washington Examiner, 9/8/10, Virginia congressman admits: 'If you don't tie our hands, we will keep stealing.' (http://www.washingtonexaminer.com/opinion/blogs/beltway-confidential/virginia-congressman-admits-if-you-dont-tie-our-hands-we-will-keep-stealing-102466389.html)

***Sign On San Diego, 12/5/05, Lawmaker keeps wife on payroll(http://www.signonsandiego.com/uniontrib/20051204/news_1m4filner.html)

****Wall Street Journal, 10/11/10, Capitol Hill's Stock Trading: What the Academic Research Concludes (http://blogs.wsj.com/deals/2010/10/11/capitol-hills-stock-trading-what-the-academic-research-concludes/)

Old Wisdom

As novel and revolutionary as today's politicians and talking heads make the concept seem, there was a time when leaders understood that government was a force to be controlled and limited.

It was common knowledge that the more good intentioned people and ambitious politicians teamed up to 'make things better', unintended consequences would follow the new wisdom of the day.

This hit home when I started doing some research into historical figures and their beliefs.   John Stuart Mill, Thomas Paine, Benjamin Franklin - all wrote great works on the rights and responsibilities of the individual and the need to limit government control.

But the idea that man should be left to find his own path, free of government help or meddling, was put best by a person who truly knew the value of liberty:

> *I have had but one answer from the beginning. Do nothing with us! Your doing with us has already played the mischief with us. Do nothing with us! If the apples will not remain on the tree of their own strength, if they are wormeaten at the core, if they are early ripe and disposed to fall, let them fall!*

The speaker is Frederick Douglass, giving a speech in 1865 called 'What the Black Man Wants.'   The question being answered is 'What shall we do with the Negro?', a hot topic at the end of the Civil War.

Here was a man who was born and raised a slave, ran North to freedom, and built himself up to the point where had the ear of

15

the President of the United States while the nation was walking back from near total collapse.

The power he held to direct what would become of the freed slaves and what the government would do to help these newly emancipated people is difficult to put into words.

Yet with all that power, when asked how the freed slaves should be treated, his own life taught him a lesson that was simple and direct - give people liberty and the respect due all free men. Stop trying to 'help' people by controlling their lives.

Mr. Douglass knew that in order for his people to rise from bondage they needed the freedom to be in charge of their own destiny. If a man is rotten let him fall, but given the opportunity to fight for his own success,

> *"he will fight," as Mr. Quincy, our President, said, in earlier days than these, "when there is reasonable probability of his whipping anybody."*

As a society, we have been through this battle many times since. People of means and ambition coupled with true believers of a 'better way' continue to take on the task of engineering a better nation through programs, regulations, assistance, and compassionate intervention.

People with good intentions and dreams of power have outlawed intoxicants one decade and subsidized drug and alcohol habits the next through welfare and public housing.

They've taxed and regulated tobacco while subsidizing obesity and the processed food industry. They create special rights for certain criminals and illegal immigrants while restricting the rights of citizens to protect themselves from predators... and all in the name of progress, justice, and equality.

No matter where you look, where big problems have stayed the same or gotten worse, you will find government making a mess and ever more excuses, demanding ever greater resources to 'address' the same problem they never fix.

That's not to say that government has no role in society, or that people should have the freedom to do anything they want with no consequences.

But when people use the power of government to attempt to force society to standards that are impossible to objectively measure - standards such as morality, compassion, welfare, health, and self esteem for starters - then you necessarily trample the rights of one segment of society for the benefit of another, more preferred segment.

That may work great for politicians, who gain ever more access to our money, which they in turn hand out to their favored friends and vote wranglers.

Yet their efforts erode our freedom, ingenuity, and the ability of the citizens to better their lives the only way they truly can - on their own.

Their efforts also, in what would seem to be a contradiction, do great damage to the institution of government itself.

The more you have under government control, the more corruption becomes inevitable. The more government fails to cure the problems they take responsibility for, the less people have faith in the nature, direction, and purpose of government.

Being left to deal with the problems as individuals and as a society, separate from government, is the only solution.

The daily give and take of life will serve as a living laboratory for individual growth; learning from our mistakes and picking ourselves back up again will make us stronger; and taking responsibility for helping our neighbors and community will bring us together.

We need to regain the freedom to fail so that we can all have the opportunity to succeed.

I must say, I love the 'freedom to fail' line so much I wanted to it use as my subtitle, but it's everywhere, from books to essays to articles already, and I'm not nearly cool enough to pull off 'trendy'. But that's not important right now.

What's important is realizing that we need politicians to stop taking away the right of the individual to control his own fate, stop allowing lobbyists and aides decide how much control we will have over our own lives, and change the relationship between the people who have achieved prosperity and those who need help out of desperate and dangerous circumstances.

Nobody is Entitled

It's a sad reality of life that there are people in need, both in the poorest and richest countries around the world. Poverty is a disease that has been battled for centuries, but refuses to die.

Tragedy strikes families, companies, and industries all the time, leaving people behind to suffer under the strain of lives shattered. People make mistakes that cost their families peace, security, stability - and if the mistake is big enough it can affect an entire generation.

It is here, among the hard times that hit us all eventually, that government has fought the longest running and most well financed battles in my lifetime, and where we spend every single dollar that the US government brings in from income taxes.

No, that is not an exaggeration. Our current federal obligations to Social Security, Medicare, and Medicaid gobble up the entire tax base of the United States of America. The rest is borrowed.*

This isn't the sum total of what we spend on social programs aimed at fighting poverty directly (food stamps, welfare, section 8 housing and other housing assistance, etc.), but these 'third rails' of politics have grown to the point where it takes every dime we pay through income taxes to support them.

The creation of these programs - sold as just a little something to help those in need - was done with the support of the American people. We voted in the representatives, Senators, and Presidents who created, expanded, and managed these programs into the unwieldy beasts they have become.

Since their inception, corruption, fraud, mismanagement, and the unquenchable lust for power have pushed these apparatus of poverty abatement into every corner of our lives, searching for more and more resources to throw at a problem that refuses go away, and our fearless spenders are coming up with ever more ways to keep the fight alive.

19

This year, in spite of widespread public opposition and a continued, growing desire to repeal the law that created it, the Affordable Care Act (aka Obamacare) was passed as part of the battle against hardship.

It is part one of a plan to create universal health care, and is the first bill to ever force citizens to buy a particular product (insurance), a major expansion of the role of government in our daily lives.

Will this latest attempt to deal with the scourge of poverty do anything to make the poorest among us equal in health to those who have health insurance today?

The experience in Europe and Canada, where healthcare has been universal for decades, says no.   The British National Health Service in particular is a great source of ammunition for those opposed to universal healthcare in the US.

Long lines for treatment, a severe shortage of doctors and nurses, wages and benefits mandated by the government, routinely botched surgeries and infant deliveries, and even the recent story of a man who died of thirst** while in a British hospital speaks to the amazing lack of quality that comes with a public health bureaucracy.

Not to say that people living in those counties with universal healthcare don't have options.

Canadians routinely purchase private health insurance... that can only be used in US hospitals, where they come for treatment.

The provincial governor of Newfoundland even flew to the US for heart surgery because he wanted the best, and Canada didn't have anything comparable to the quality of medical care offered south of the border.***

But even if those stories weren't out there, the reason we were told there was a 'moral imperative' to provide coverage to the uninsured was the skyrocketing cost of insurance coverage and healthcare services.

What was never discussed in the process of bashing through this new entitlement were the reasons why health insurance is out of reach for most people.

The first and simplest explanation is that it isn't. Health insurance may not be cheap, but there was already a wide variety of coverage options that are very affordable to someone at or near the poverty line.

The decision to limit other expenses that you find in the homes of Americans above and below the poverty line - multiple televisions, cars, entertainment devices, drugs, alcohol, etc. - would be necessary, but if someone chooses to forgo health coverage to buy something else, it is their decision that put themselves in peril, not society's.

I made the decision go without health insurance myself when I was in my mid-20's, and suffered through a few separated shoulders and a recurring knee injury without treatment before I decided to change my financial priorities - and stop playing rugby.

The second is that Medicaid - which already provides healthcare coverage to the poor and disabled, as well as illegal immigrants, people who lie about having insurance when they go in for minor emergencies, etc. - drives up costs by absorbing hospital resources, creating a new layer of bureaucracy, and paying at a lower rate than actual costs, increasing prices as the rest of us cover the shortfall that Medicaid - and its sibling program Medicare - create.

These costs are absorbed by hospitals, who have to charge higher fees, and insurance providers who have to pay those higher fees along with their staff to handle the process.

So when you look at the basis of expensive insurance, you have to see the reality behind the uninsured.

The first reason may be short sighted and irresponsible individuals, but the second is all about government intervention. Social programs are a major driver of increased cost. So what does government do to deal with the problem their programs created?

Add more government!

To deal with the first factor- the one where people choose not to buy insurance, exercising their own freedom of choice - they decide that everybody has to buy insurance, unless they fall into the special categories of people exempt from this requirement - members of select unions and government employees are two prime examples.

Of course, since our politicians know that forcing people in poverty to buy insurance would be a strain on their wallets - the reason they didn't buy insurance in the first place - it threw in other exemptions for people below a certain multiple of the poverty line (which can always be changed later to expand/ contract to cover the favored and punish the opposed) so that they don't really have to pay anything.

Those who choose not to take care of their own needs get the freebies, the politicians get votes, and those who actually take responsibility for their own lives pick up the check.

This isn't conjecture - the new regulations actually demand that those who pay for their own health care pay more in a variety of ways.

With the new Affordable Care Act, not only has the cost of health insurance premiums gone up, but the number of items you can buy with pre-tax dollars has shrunk, and any employer-paid insurance premiums will be reported directly to the IRS - so that when the system goes broke, they can tax your health benefits as income.

But that's not the worst of it.

While the new laws increase costs to those who pay, they also expand the class of dependents in society - people who either forget or never develop the ability to take care of themselves - by way government largesse.

Eventually, via the increasing demands by those receiving government assistance, the activists and bureaucrats that are paid to administrate and distribute that assistance, and the fact that none of the money or services received is ever paid back by the recipients, those who receive unearned benefits believe they are entitled to both funds and services, and encouraged to see themselves as due these entitlements by elected leaders and activists who control the purse strings.

The end result of the entitlement mentality was put most eloquently by a rather famous immigrant - President Obama's Aunt Zeituni, in her September 2010 interview with WBZ-TV in Boston, where she lived for 10 years in public housing, at least 6 of those years while ignoring a deportation order:

> *"I didn't ask for it; they gave it to me. Ask your system. I didn't create it or vote for it. Go and ask your system," she said unapologetically.*

> *"I didn't take any advantage of the system. The system took advantage of me."*

> *"To me America's dream became America's worst nightmare," she said adamantly. "I have been treated like public enemy number one."*

That last line really cracks me up, since she attended her nephew's 2005 inauguration as a junior State Senator in Illinois, and his Presidential inauguration in 2008. If that's how public enemies are treated these days, we've really got to review those Secret Service protocols.

Yet her words betray an attitude that isn't rare in parts of our nation.

The attitude states that people are due benefits, and services, and housing, and food, and even spending cash because while this country is rich, they and their friends are not. The attitude breeds resentment, recrimination, and desires for societal revenge.

From this attitude eternal victims are born.

*Instapundit, 7/12/10, DEBT IS A CANCER (http://pajamasmedia.com/instapundit/102757/)

**The Guardian (UK), 3/6/10, Neglected by 'lazy' nurses, man, 22, dying of thirst rang the police to beg for water (http://www.dailymail.co.uk/news/article-1255858/Neglected-lazy-nurses-Kane-Gorny-22-dying-thirst-rang-police-beg-water.html)

***National Post (Canada), 2/1/10, N.L. Premier Williams set to have heart surgery in U.S. (http://www.nationalpost.com/news/story.html?id=2510700)

From Victorious to Victimized

To see oneself as an eternal victim is dangerous to the individual and the society at large. Victims feel separate, different, alone. They don't have to follow the same rules as everyone else because they have suffered somehow, somewhere.

The offense didn't even have to happen to them personally. Perceived historical wrongs of racism, anti-communism, sexism, capitalism, colonialism, or some other -ism are often to blame.

The key to the victim's thinking lies in the belief that the problems of individuals and that of the nation were created by some nefarious forces dominating the land.

It doesn't take a whole river of data to see where the idea of victimhood is most widespread. The public housing projects and Section 8 districts of every major city are filled with people and their advocates ready to tell you that the situation of the poor is not their fault.

They were raised in poverty, it's all they know.

They couldn't do well in public school - the other kids beat up people who stand out.

They had to join a gang - it's the only way to survive.

They can't get a job - nobody will hire a gangbanger, ex-con, or dropout for anything worth doing, and you don't get any respect for flipping burgers, taking out the trash, or washing dishes.

Even if they tried to rise up and out of their situation, society will never allow them to go anywhere.

If it sounds familiar, that's because we hear variations of the above from every civil rights leader, activist group, and politician when the discussing people and places where things never seem to get better - the inner cities, the Alleghenies, Reno, etc.

While living in these neighborhoods myself at a few stages in life, I heard the laments of victimhood in the bodegas, the street corners, and the bars as people looked for reasons why their lives didn't measure up to those lucky bastards living it up elsewhere.

Even people who rise from poverty to luxury feel the need to reassert their victim status.

That's how we got from the color-blind dreams of Martin Luther King to the 'Half-a-mil for bail cause I'm African' lament of Jay-Z*, who has become a mega-millionaire selling the idea of rebellion while taking full advantage of what America offers - opportunity open to all who have the talent, drive, ambition, and will to take advantage of it.

The fade of Martin's dream follows the path of good intentions that ignored his call for a color-blind society and the plea of Frederick Douglass to leave people alone to succeed or fail on their own, and replaced it with a mission to come to the rescue of those who were perceived to be too flawed to survive.

That is, was, and will always be the message of 'public assistance' - We have to be there because some people just can't be trusted to make it on their own.

It's a self-fulfilling prophecy as people who live surrounded by self identified victims never see opportunity - they are constantly exposed to failure and are told that they will never have a chance to succeed.

The people who rise to power around the eternal victims always seem to be those who are most wrapped up in the process of making sure that nobody is allowed to be without some form of public assistance.

26

Yet the fact remains that all the money in the world cannot solve the problem of poverty and unequal outcomes in life. Not everyone can be successful, not everyone can be wealthy, not everyone can be powerful.

Somebody, often through the consequence of their own decisions, is going to be poor. The more we spend to shield people from the consequences of their actions, the more likely they are to continue to, if I may be blunt, do stupid things and make stupid decisions that will reinforce their poverty.

But that's not to say that something can't be done to help people who are willing to ask for it.

I use the word 'help' because 'assistance' - that which the public provides - is a crutch or a handrail, something that gets you through, but never makes actually fixes the problem that necessitated the assistance in the first place.

Help is geared toward actually solving problems, and is what one gets when they seek it, and it is given voluntarily.

The result of being assisted is relief, while the result of being helped is gratitude.

The amazing thing about help is that it benefits both sides of the equation. The giver knows they did something good, and feel better about themselves, and often seeks other ways to help more people.

The recipient knows that there are other people out there willing to help, and if they do appreciate the help, they will try to pay back that help by either working to improve their situation, helping the person who previously helped them, or helping someone else.

The reason why all this works is because even in the absence of government assistance, people want to be there for people in need. Shocking, I know.

But the fact is Americans are the most generous people on the planet, without taking into account the foreign aid our government sends around the world to buy allies and influence the rest.

We have earned our place as the world's most generous nation because when somebody near or far needs help, the American people send more money, manpower, food, and aid than anyone else. When tragedy strikes around the globe, it is the American people who come to the rescue.

When people need help here at home, we offer it most effectively person to person through what used to be a noble pursuit, but has become somewhat of a dirty word since the government took over responsibility for dealing with every social ill imaginable.

The word is 'charity', and the receipt of it has managed to become something to be ashamed of, the giving of it sign of arrogance and elitism.

Sad, because prior to the 1960s, charity was how people took care of each other, and it was amazingly effective in getting help to those who need it and allowing those who wanted to help their neighbors do so effectively and efficiently.

The people who used to receive charity both appreciated the help and worked to repay those who gave it to them.

Those people on the receiving end that didn't appreciate the help, never improved their own situation, or refused to take responsibility for their own lives no longer received help. Built in protection from people who choose to mooch rather than contribute!

Private charity is designed to help people get beyond the point of needing help if they are able, care for the indigent who can no longer care for themselves, and - especially those charities that stem from religious institutions - create a sense that we are all in this together, part of something larger.

The history of charity is filled with evidence that a network of individually operated private charities - secular, religious, corporate sponsored, local food pantry, whatever - are far superior to anything the government can do.

Average Genius at work, as the people get together to deal with a problem, with a long history of success.

It seems obvious that if you were a political leader looking for ways to help citizens in need, the first thing to be done would be to raise the limits on charitable tax deductions, allowing people to choose who should receive their generosity and encouraging people to seek out private charities to donate to.

Yet in one of the first declarations of his administration, our former community organizer President made it clear he would be reducing the tax deduction for charitable giving** so that the federal government could use the additional money for its own purposes.

This preference for government run assistance programs is due to the greatest unspoken weakness of private charity - that there are limited opportunities to use it for political ends.

Government run public assistance is designed to build allegiances between the dependents receiving the aid, the staff administrating it, and the politicians who took our money to fund it.

Nowhere in the government equation is there a focus on getting people off the dole, reducing the amount of resources dedicated to 'addressing the problem', or creating a sense that we are all in this together.

Just the opposite, since the whole notion of public assistance is built upon the idea that money has to be taken from the wealthy,

29

the middle class, and the working folks to continually fund the assistance apparatus.

Its almost as if some people - highly educated, separated from the realities of everyday life, driven to expand their power - are either blind or ignorant to the fact that government is much more adept at causing than fixing the problems of the common man. They have either forgotten or ignored the wisdom of Frederick Douglass.

That's not to say that the government should be completely absent from helping alleviate poverty. There are areas where government could be a productive force for helping those in need.

First, the government has the power of investigation and law enforcement. That power could be used to ensure that charities distribute the funds to those who need it and do not use those funds primarily for 'administrative' costs. This kind of oversight is sorely needed.

Recent revelations concerning the ONE Foundation, an anti-global poverty charity founded by Bono of the band U2, found that of the $12.8 million it received in donations, only 1.2% actually went to charity.*** The rest went to salaries and efforts to 'raise awareness'.

I'm pretty sure people already were 'aware' of poverty and the need to help those experiencing it's effects, so it would be wise for some institution to step in and make sure the funds start going to the needy, not the sanctimonious publicity hounds.

Government can't seem do that for the assistance programs it runs now, resulting in stories of waste, fraud, mismanagement, and embezzlement every few months.

If we build a system that separates the giving of aid from those making sure the process is done without fraud or favoritism - where each side has a clear purpose instead of the whole enterprise being subject to the corruption of politics - the whole process will run with more transparency and efficiency.

Second, as mentioned, the government could raise the amount of money people could write off as charitable deductions on their taxes.

Give people the power and encouragement to designate who will benefit from their hard work. If they choose not to take advantage of that opportunity, so be it. But at least give them the option.

This will benefit everyone, and since donations to churches are among the most common across the economic spectrum, it will help rebuild institutions that make members of society better people.

Third, government agencies that currently administer assistance can be streamlined, downsized, and used to direct people to private organizations there to help people get past temporary issues and get treatment for permanent problems.

The people currently working those agencies tasked with providing 'assistance' would clearly be first in line to start working with the private charities, and wouldn't be hamstrung by the currently public regulations designed to propagate poverty and may actually find themselves in a position to help alleviate it.

Most importantly, by connecting the people needing help to those giving it, the people receiving help would, on the whole, see the generosity of their neighbors, develop a sense of gratitude, and stop seeing themselves as 'entitled' to benefits.

None of this will end poverty, stop the drug trade, the existence of gangs, or the dangerous and evil decisions of the stupid, ignorant, short sighted, or lazy. But it will slow the spreading disease of victimhood through segments of society that don't need any more obstacles than life already throws at us.

If you want to know why I'm sure this will work, I know from personal experience that the most effective way to rise from poverty to stability and eventually (hopefully) prosperity is to accept responsibility for past mistakes, build your own future, and appreciate the blessing of having people around that are willing to help.

Look around your own world and see how many success stories started with that formula somewhere along the way.

*Jay-Z, The Black Album (2004), 99 Problems (a great song, btw)

**The Chronicle of Philanthropy, 2/26/09, Obama's Plan to Reduce Charitable Deductions for the Wealthy Draws Criticism (http://philanthropy.com/article/Obamas-Plan-to-Reduce/63024/)

***The Vile Plutocrat, 9/24/10, Bono's ONE Foundation Poverty Initiative Gave Only 1% to Charity, (https://thevileplutocrat.com/bile/articles/bonos-one-foundation-poverty-initiative-gave-only-1-to-charity/)

The Amazing Race to the Bottom

Nowhere has the intervention of government been more damaging than in relations between the races in America, and the more direct the intervention, the more far reaching and harder to overcome that damage has been.

I don't want to ignore that fact that racism exists.

It does, it always will, and it will always be most prevalent among the poor, the ignorant, and those who want to control people that seek absolution from their own failures. But true racism is not what government agencies and activists fight, and not why the race industry thrives on government subsistence.

Programs, concepts, and prejudices against individual liberty that started in universities have branched out into mainstream culture at an alarming pace, and all are based on the idea that racism is so bad that only something as powerful as government can stop it.

To reinforce this idea, a lot of groups have become de-facto racism police, out in force to make sure we all know that race is the hidden motivation of nearly every decision made by millions of people, every day.

This is evident in exceedingly vocal accusations of racism by groups that are nominally focused on 'civil rights', 'equality', and 'social justice'.

The racism they cite - even unproven, completely manufactured controversies where a singular sign at a protest or a bigoted comment that isn't seen or heard by anyone else - is sold as proof that the world is unfair to people of color.

On the other hand, the racism of a 'civil rights' leader, progressive/liberal/Democrat politician, bureaucrat, celebrity or pundit who happens to be of color is just part of that person's expression and a result of.... the racism directed at them!

The worst offenders are the civil rights organizations that populate cable news shows - African American organizations like the NAACP and the New Black Panther Party; hispanic organizations like La Raza and MeCha; muslim organizations like CAIR.

All of these groups send people out in front of the protest when someone may have possibly offended their people, and double back to excuse the offense when one of their leaders or political allies is exposed as a bigot.

My favorite examples involve the politicians these groups support. Just this year, numerous Democrat politicians made inflammatory and racist statements, and were shielded by groups supposedly dedicated bridging racial divides.

The most egregious was the interview Loretta Sanchez, D-CA, gave to the Univision television network regarding her opponent for a congressional seat, Van Tran, who is Vietnamese. In this Spanish language interview, she said that the Vietnamese were trying to steal the Latino people's seat in Congress*.

Given that her district includes a very large number of Vietnamese people - Little Saigon of the L.A. basin is there - this would seem to be not only inflammatory, but a clear example of discriminating against a minority segment of her constituency. So much for inclusiveness.

La Raza and MeCha's reaction to blatant racism? Silence. It was racism from their side, so it's just an expression of ethnic solidarity.

Other examples include Paul Jankorski (D-PA), whose statement about the stimulus deserves a full block quote:

> *"We're giving relief to people that I deal with in my office every day now unfortunately. But because of the longevity of this recession, these are people — and*

they'   re not minorities and they're not defective and
they'   re not all the things you'd like to insinuate that these
    programs are about — these are average, good
American people."**

Robert Byrd (D-WV) was given a pass for being a leader and recruiter for the KKK and years of racist statements because *"He was a country boy from the hills and hollows from West Virginia. He was trying to get elected."****

Let us not forget that the same day Zoe Lofgren (D-CA) invited a comedian to add his colonoscopy to the Congressional Record, a member of the Department of Justice's Civil Rights Division testified that political appointees decided the DOJ refused to prosecute civil rights violations... that happened to white people.****

Or the judge who rejected a plea agreement because the defendant was white and he was tired of 'white boys getting off easy.'*****

The fact is, the new civil rights establishment is designed to keep people separate, not bring them together. Race driven court decisions, funding decisions, quotas, and programs exacerbate the sense of 'us vs. them', creating conflicts where none need exist.

This is how things work when government bureaucrats get to decide how to make race relations better. They completely miss the mark.

We can do better. In fact, we do better everyday, on our own, by going out into the real world, earning a living.

My own experience is a great illustration. I began working working weekends and summers early in my high school days, and when I got to college, worked full time to pay for what my loans didn't cover.

I worked in pet stores, the campus cafeteria, restaurants, bars, construction, and a variety of other odd jobs to earn extra money and pay my way through school and continued to hold second jobs for extra cash when I started my career.

The people I worked with were of every race, creed, and color. Some were liberals/progressives/hippies. Some were conservative future tycoons. Some were immigrants, transplants, burnouts, and roustabouts.

All of us - in every job - were taking responsibility for ourselves and the world around us. We eventually left those jobs learning something about other people, without any racial or economic hatred developing.

From what I experienced, people respected each other, understanding that individuals are different and not blaming things on generalizations or stereotypes.

Relations weren't perfect - conflict is inevitable when you mix humans together - but there was no sense that anyone was more special than anyone else for any reasons other than personal ones.

When you hated someone you worked with, it was for a good reason, not some theory on the role of race in the assignment of shifts, sections, or really crappy cooking duties.

Even in the construction industry - not known for it's enlightened workforce - people tended to move up and around based on their skills.

Race relations would be far better today if only the advice of Frederick Douglass had been heeded. Hate arises from ignorance, privilege, and separation. Real life is full of coexistence and cooperation, and that can't be forced.

Putting the government in charge and allowing them to take responsibility for dealing with racism only serves to make the problem worse, which is why the worst racism found by those looking is typically involves government - and then among those aligned with the racial grievance theater patrons.

That's not to say that people outside of government agencies are without prejudice, always make the right call, are the best and most moral of people, or without flaw. But an individual's ignorance and prejudice can't do nearly the damage of government policy and institutions.

We have proof of that all around us, as a combination of racial power brokering and 'compassion' shows that institutional bigotry has the potential to damage millions of lives.

*CBS News, 9/24/10, Loretta Sanchez: "The Vietnamese" are Trying to Take My Seat (http://www.cbsnews.com/8301-503544_162-20017604-503544.html)

**Hot Air, 6/24/10, Dem Rep says "minorities, defective[s]" not "average, good American people" (http://hotair.com/archives/2010/06/24/dem-rep-says-minorities-defectives-not-average-good-american-people/)

***American Thinker, 7/4/10, A Clinton Entendre Eulogy (http://www.americanthinker.com/2010/07/a_clinton_entendre_eulogy.html)

**** Powerline, 9/23/10, Christopher Coates Takes the Stand (http://www.powerlineblog.com/archives/2010/09/027302.php)

*****MSNBC, 10/6/10, Black judge rejects plea deal for 'white boy' (http://www.msnbc.msn.com/id/39536917/ns/us_news/)

Birds of a Feather Flocking Things Up

In Southern California, the inability/unwillingness to secure our southern border has transformed large sections of the Los Angles basin, along with sections of every major city in the country, into nearly separate countries.

There are neighborhoods, even whole towns, where English is largely unspoken. The labor market in some areas is near majority undocumented - people who are here illegally, living and working in as separate an existence as they can have outside of prison.

For the unscrupulous businessmen and criminals who thrive in areas where laws are flexible or ignored, it is hard to find a better environment to grow. A large population of people who can't get legal work creates a black market for labor, and the financial incentives to break the law far outweigh the cost of getting caught.

A large number of people living in fear, actively avoiding law enforcement? Just install a giant 'Welcome Home!' sign to criminal enterprises and embrace reality.

Politicians benefit too, buying votes by creating services for those with low declared incomes, and creating jobs for bureaucrats hired to administrate the dole. They then turn a blind eye to exploited illegal work force, not to mention the drug mules, pushers, and addicts. Their jobs are as invested in the atmosphere of lawlessness as anyone else.

Of course the circus wouldn't be complete without 'civil rights' leaders to tell the rest of the us how horrible we are for trying to clean things up.

Wanting our government to enforce border security; anger at businesses hiring people who can't legally work here; despair at seeing what were once thriving middle and working class neighborhoods turned into a separate nation run by gangs and cartels - it must be racism!

Now, the rise of ethnic neighborhoods are nothing new, and if those areas serve as a transition point for immigrants to assimilate to their new nation, that's a good thing - especially since that tends to be where you find the best in ethnic cuisines.

Anyone who has seen me eat understands that I'm never against improving available food options.

But that's not what is happening with massive illegal immigration. Illegal immigration creates a society that is not only separate, but set up in opposition to the rest of the nation while being dependent upon 'community leaders' to provide even the most basic of needs, and in a state of constant fear in a land where they can barely communicate with its legal citizens.

The effect of the soft amnesties of the 90's and lack of immigration law enforcement eventually created two sets of dependents; the unskilled citizens out of work and the dependent illegal immigrant who would have to vote, legally or not, for government largesse if they wanted to keep getting free services and lax immigration enforcement.

The damage doesn't end with the illegal immigrant community and the unskilled citizens. The border towns have become wholly owned territories of the drug cartels and smugglers that took power over the ports of entry.

People are forced to take drugs, weapons, and laundered money across as payment to the 'coyotes' who lead them through the deserts; murder, kidnappings and beheadings are rampant on both sides of the border; and everyone from police to military to prison guards and wardens are given a choice - take a bribe or a hail of bullets towards them and their family.

The borderlands weren't always like this, and the rise of drug smuggling and border violence matched - in scale and timing -

the rise of sanctuary cities, social services for illegal immigrants, and the decision to stop actively enforcing border security.

The rise of citizens groups to push for enforcement of the immigration laws and increase border security have changed the debate in this nation, because our political leaders and academics - largely separated from the results of their policies - didn't seriously consider the damages of not enforcing the border.

All the leaders, activists, and academics see are people for the activists to 'speak for' and the Chamber of Commerce to exploit.

The Average Genius of the citizenry will continue to be the only effective leadership in solving the problem. We understand that governing based on compassion and a perverted definition of justice has managed to create, in the span of two generations, a far reaching destruction to the same people the activists claim they are helping.

We also understand that poor, unskilled, undereducated immigrants and citizens of this country continue to be crippled by these policies. Nobody wins except the wealthy and those in a position to take advantage of this new, dependence based society.

Which is a great lead in for the next subject.

Consequences, Intended and Unintended

Similar to what happened with race relations, immigration, and the 'war on poverty' in all it's forms, the result of government interference into home ownership wasn't peace, prosperity and happiness but greater power for those in, around, and aligned with government interests.

It didn't have to be like this.   The initial intervention was designed to ensure people weren't being turned down for loans because of their race - which needed to be done. But it turned into a policy of forcing banks to lend money to people who couldn't afford to pay it back.

Government meddling took an industry that had built up reserves and defenses to deal with wildly varying economic cycles being given a mix of positive and negative incentives to abandon all reason and put everything on the line for one big boom, and a government agency created to help first time homebuyers eventually guaranteeing over 90% of the nation's mortgages.*

The bust this boom begat was far more damaging than those of the past. The early 90's housing crash in California following the closure of the military bases (yep, that crisis was caused by government too!) caused a 30% 'correction' in housing prices across the state. This crash caused a 50% drop in home values in San Diego County alone. So far.

Left to pick up the pieces are a lot of pissed off people who are either underwater on their mortgage or dealing with foreclosure; a massive increase in the unemployed and a major decrease in the number of people considered 'in the workforce'; and people who still have jobs looking at big tax increases to pay for the bailouts and programs to fix the problems they created.

The housing industry grew steadily and without major upheaval for decades before the government stepped in, and should have been left alone to do the same. But no, the true believers and politicians knew better.

As with all government action, this failure had some collateral damage, and the housing collapse didn't just affect home prices or the bailed out banks holding bad mortgages.

Because getting a loan was easier and far faster then building savings, people were refinancing to take advantage of their quickly growing equity, buying all sorts of toys - boats, electronics, and especially new cars.   The manufacturers ramped up production, and when the money stopped flowing...

The car companies took the crash like a left hook. Beyond the excess inventory, they also had union labor contracts and an aggressive field of competitors.   Money they borrowed when times were good came due, they couldn't give away their inventory, and the financing companies they owned were stuck with a whole lot of repossessions and people falling behind on payments.

The future for the Big 3 American car companies was so dark they needed a miner's cap just to see the options.

Those options broke down like this - liquidate and go out of business, figure out how to get your financial house in order and take a hit now, or take a government loan and give the feds some control over your business.

Two of the Big 3 took the government option, taking a bailout to pay their bills and attempt to dig their way out of a hole, to quote President Obama.

But there's a problem - as anyone who has found themselves in a hole knows, you can't dig your way out, you need to start climbing.

GM and Chrysler's leadership never learned that lesson. They chose the government option and left us, the taxpayers who now own the company, with stark lessons in how government good deeds lead to corruption.

GM was not only bailed out, but their debt and ownership was literally taken from their investors and given to the unions - who had a major impact on getting the current leadership into office.

The company now has to ask Congress before making any moves toward profitability. To purchase a subprime lender that our other bailouts didn't manage to save, GM had to go and beg Congress for the right to purchase the ailing bank to replace GMAC, which was sold in the bankruptcy that their own bailout couldn't stave off.

That permission is needed because in spite of the accounting trick that allowed GMs president to claim the bailout was paid back, the company still owes a few billion in TARP cash to the government, so the strings are still pulled by our fearless lenders in Congress.

The level of control the G-Men have was made clear when this same gentleman suggested that the treasury sell it's shares so that GM could stop being called 'Government Motors'. He was fired a week later.

Of course, in spite of it's standing as a government owned entity, GM is still allowed to donate to political campaigns. Nothing says 'keep the bailout funds flowing' like donations to the leadership of both major political parties and complete obedience when the White House decides leadership needs a'changing!

Chrysler had it's own set of issues, as it was sold off to Fiat, adding some international intrigue into the mix. This deal was even dirtier than the GM fiasco, especially since their bondholders - people who paid top dollar to invest in the company to insure that if things went south, they would be paid first - were forced to take a 95% cut in their investment.

In addition to cutting out the investors, dealerships for both manufacturers had their agreements cancelled and locations closed on orders of the government installed leadership.

A recent report by an independent investigator found that the decisions about who would keep their stores - and whose employees would be forced onto the unemployment lines - were based not on their history or financial position, but the gender, race, and political affiliation of the owners.

Sit back and consider that for a moment. Two companies were absorbed by the government, and ownership rights were taken away from investors and handed off as a political payout. Competitors at the street level were either allowed to stay in business or forced to shut down based on their connection to the political party in power.

Patronage usually means giving government jobs to your political allies, supporters, and staff. Ambassadorships, department head positions, staff assignments, even jobs making foreign and domestic policy.

Now we have entire corporations being handed off to the people who in turn provide money, votes, and power to those doling out the goodies. The people who didn't support the political leadership were shut down.

Not everyone took the easy way out. Ford decided to pass on the government bailout and deal with the problems they created over the previous decades. They took a hit, restructured their debt, and changed the way they do business in the plants.

Taking responsibility for their own success paid off. Their sales have rebounded dramatically, the public perception of the company is rock solid, and their investors didn't get shafted in favor of political operatives, activists, and union leadership.

Ford also didn't have dealerships shut down because the owners were members of the wrong color, gender, or political groups. Dealerships closed, but those decisions were made by the market based on their ability to stay profitable.

Just like businesses that close down every day, the decision to close was made based on business reasons, not directed by government lackeys to pay off their political donors and allies.

Looking back at the collapse of other industries in American history - those that were not phased out of relevance by advancing technology - it's clear that increasing government regulation, interference, and control was at the heart of the failures.

Manufacturing in this country is in retreat not because of foreign competition alone, but because the employee unions were given government backing to shut down plants if they didn't get far more pay than the company was able to afford when foreign competition arose.

Increased costs created by new regulation played their part too, adding fees for lawyers, insurance, taxes, government mandated pensions, increased benefits, environmental compliance reports... the list goes on and on.

Currently the cost of regulations is 14% of our national income. 14% of the money we spend goes to the government in the forms of regulatory fees. This does not include taxes - it's pure cost added to the price of products and services before they even reach the shelves.**

The imposition of each and every new fee, regulation, and tax was meant to correct a perceived injustice perpetrated on the rest of society - to make the companies pay for 'exploiting' their workers, i.e. being successful.

With each new regulation/law/tax/fee, companies cut back on other costs, cut workers, and eventually find their way to greener pastures - at first in other states that actually want the jobs, and then to other countries as the nation's leaders - who continue to develop new and exciting ways to take - make the country more and more hostile to anyone who has the drive and initiative to create.

The point of all this is too demonstrate that by giving government control over the daily workings of business - even if the reasons for that control are as compassionate as 'trying to help people feel the joys of home ownership' or 'trying to save thousands of jobs in a vital industry' - winds up becoming not just a huge mess, but a corrupt mess where the politically connected get richer and more powerful, and everyone else gets screwed.

And while the most recent and egregious examples were thrust upon us by Democrats, the Republicans are only better by degree.

The reason why Republicans lost control of the both houses of Congress in the election of 2006 was because they spent billions of taxpayer dollars on their allies through the earmark process, where the spending isn't directly approved, just added to other bills to 'ease passage'.

I'm quite certain that just like the spending and influence peddling done by the Democrats, the Republicans believed with all their heart that every dollar spent and every project approved was vital to the health of their communities. That fact that it helped build support and gain votes was just a happy accident.

However, every new project, every new expansion of government power and influence, and every new restriction on individual liberty blazed a trail for the less angelic souls in Washington to take advantage of the newly created powers for their own gain.

It's the great tragedy of our times, the story of compassion and emotion driving our leadership, and the processes being overtaken and abused for the gain of the powerful and the connected.

That's assuming that the compassion is real and the corruption came along as an unwanted passenger.

The more cynical view - a point of view that can only be proved by a look inside the hearts and minds of those in power - is that the corruption and power lead the way while compassion and justice are trotted out as sales tools.

We can't look inside the hearts of others, so instead of accusing people of things that can't be proven, instead it's left to us to decide - the voters, the taxpayers, and the people who are given the ultimate power to select who will be given the honor of representing us - what type of leadership is the most beneficial for the nation, the community, and the protection of all of our individual rights.

When it comes to our economy, allowing companies and individuals to work without the influence and power of government forcing them to move in one direction or another is the best choice.

Corruption is enough of a problem without giving our leaders new and exciting of avenues for patronage, graft, and abuse of office.

The government's role needs to be limited, defined, and directed at protecting our rights. Taking their eyes off that specific and essentially directive allows the idle hands of the wealthy, privileged, connected and powerful to get us all into real trouble as they try yet again to 'do something with us.'

I don't mean to sound like a talking-pointing spouting cable news pundit, but the result of this latest round of government driven destruction should be anything and everything except more government control.

Regulation should be limited to creating and maintaining laws that keep people from being cheated. Government needs to be an umpire or a referee, not a player/manager/umpire/commissioner and executioner all at the same time.

We also need to figure out where to draw the line between where we do and do not not want the law to tread. Kevin D. Williamson of the National Review has a suggestion:

'If you're not willing to have somebody hauled off at gunpoint over the project, then it's probably not a legitimate concern of the state.'***

Without a simple understanding of where the limits of government power need to be drawn, the politicians and their surrogates will continue to expand their reach past our wallets and further into our lives.

Allowing the government more power and control winds up being worse than the problems they try to fix, leaving the rest of the nation with a big mess and even bigger bill to pay for their failure.

Along with the bill for their next 'solution.'

* MarketPlace (American Public Media), 8/17/10, The Future of Fannie Mae and Freddie Mac (http://marketplace.publicradio.org/display/web/2010/08/17/pm-the-future-of-fannie-mae-and-freddie-mac/)

**Frank Holmes Instablog, 9/29/10, The Shocking Cost of Regulation (http://seekingalpha.com/instablog/389729-frank-holmes/97406-the-shocking-cost-of-regulation)

*** National Review, 9/24/10, Exchequer v. Economist (http://www.nationalreview.com/exchequer/247783/exchequer-vs-economist)

The Economics of Fail

The coming of the political season - actually, the political season doesn't end anymore, it just ebbs and flows like the tide - turns out all sorts of fun topics for discussion. The big topic is usually the economy, but healthcare moved into a close second in 2008.

The near perfect blindness of Washington to the actual results of their past decisions - aided by a media and activist community that demand our leaders 'do something!' about every problem under the sun, immediately, with no regard for past failures - means that no matter how badly both major parties have screwed things up, they feel duty bound to get their hands on some other problem that needs fixing.

This is the reason why the push for universal healthcare, healthcare reform, and the resulting Affordable Care Act referenced earlier.

Never-mind that our healthcare system was already the world's envy, with better doctors, innovation, technology, and expertise than anyone else. Never-mind that nobody was allowed to be denied healthcare, even if they had no insurance.

No, it was necessary to make sure that people who chose not to pay for healthcare had to have the same access to doctors, for any reason, at any time, as people who actually chose to devote some of their resources to their health.

The cost of healthcare itself wasn't being debated, of course. Insurance companies and doctors were declared greedy and corrupt; opposition to creating another entitlement and saddling those who paid taxes (and bought their own insurance) was deemed heartless and cruel; people who objected to the possibility of government rationed health services were derided as paranoid fanatics.

But the reasons why healthcare had become so expensive was only mentioned in passing, and even then it wasn't really clear if anyone knew how we got the point that getting sick could conceivably bankrupt a family.

The answer lies in a combination of factors, all of which designed to fix a problem, right a wrong, make things better - all good things. I spoke earlier about the insurance angle, but now let's look a little deeper.

First and foremost is innovation and personnel. Drugs need to be researched, developed, and tested. New tools don't come cheap, and somebody has to pay for the engineering, manufacturing, and distribution of these amazing new machines.

Second is liability. Lawyers get paid to sue doctors, hospitals, insurance companies, car manufacturers, the young, the elderly - basically, if there is someone who can be blamed for something, lawyers will figure out how to use the law to get paid.

Other lawyers will get paid to figure out how to keep those same people/institutions from having to pay too much. Lawyers, judges, clerks, bailiffs, notaries, the people who type on the little machines every time the lawyers are in the same room together - they all cost money too.

Everybody in this entire process adds to the cost of healthcare because every time someone dies, gets hurt, has a dispute, or is generally unhappy with something that happens in on or around a hospital, the lawyers get called in. Somebody has to carry that cost.

Which leads to the third, most prominent and least understood reason why healthcare costs so much - and insurance rears its ugly head once again.

Insurance companies have to plan for all the things that can and will go wrong, and since there are so many variables when dealing with anything that happens to the human body, they have to plan for a lawsuit every time someone gets a sniffle.

On top of that, the government of each and every state has regulated standards for what the insurance companies have to cover for everybody.

Single men pay for pre-natal care. Women pay for prostate screenings. With Medicare and Medicaid - which reimburse hospitals and doctors below the actual cost of providing care - we all pay for people who don't pay for their coverage twice, once in taxes and again through our insurance premiums.

Now, I'm not actually a heartless bastard. I want innovation - better stuff makes healthier people. I want people who need help to get it, though I think we can find a better way than just taking responsibility away from the individual. I think insurance is a good thing, though we need the ability to choose our coverage, not be told that one size will fit all when it clearly doesn't.

But if we are going to be serious about fixing the problem instead of creating another mess, we need to look at the causes, not the effects. Liability costs are a major cause. Clearly, the lawyers must die.

I kid, I kid. But we do have to do something that addresses the unscrupulous attorneys who see a piggybank in every successful company, every government program, every fender bender, and every emergency room.

You know who I'm talking about - daytime television ensures we all know that Meloni and Meloni are there for you, you may be eligible for Social Security disability benefits if you call the guy in the cowboy hat, and that Larry H. Parker got that one dude $6.1 million.

The reason why we don't already have limits on these publicity hungry, morality challenged lawyers is because they give millions upon millions of dollars to politicians to make sure that hospital regulations are impossible to live up to and damages for any suspected malpractice or negligence will be limitless.

On the other side of that equation, insurance companies find it far easier and cost effective to settle lawsuits than take their chances on a jury, especially since they have to pay the lawyers even if they win.

The bad guys - in this case the people who provide a safety net to make sure the lawyers don't just shut down hospitals when they get sued - know that some fights aren't worth getting into.

Second, people need to be able to buy the coverage they need and allow the private market to take over where there are gaps. Neighborhoods all over the country have private clinics where people can get simple help for things like rashes, food poisoning, cuts, etc.

Allowing people to buy a basic catastrophic plan, that covers almost nothing below a certain threshold, opens the door for more small clinics to step up and provide basic care for cash customers. Changing the current habit of going to the Emergency room for even the most minor of issues relieves pressure on the hospitals and frees up resources.

Couple that with some reform to the liability laws for doctors and healthcare providers and you get a reduction in insurance rates.

End restrictions on selling policies across state lines, which distort markets and create opportunities for good old fashioned influence peddling. Add in some entrepreneurs looking at a newly competitive marketplace and you have a formula for affordable healthcare.

This wouldn't provide universal coverage, and there will still be people who can't afford even the basic catastrophic insurance or a more competitive 'a la carte' plan for their family. This is where we reach back to a concept from a previous chapter - charity.

The hospitals that run as charities are numerous and legendary. St. Jude's, the Shriner's, the Ronald McDonald House - these are worthwhile institutions that do great work, providing for children in need.

There are others that do the same thing for non-children - some through churches, some driven towards specific illnesses or diseases - and all a great example of just how generous the American people are when they are asked to help.

If we really want to get healthcare to those in need and not just create another area for corruption, graft, and patronage supported by a growing vampire class sucking the nation dry, we need to make it easier to donate.

Raise the percentage of income you can deduct for charitable donations. Increase tax breaks to companies that help support charity hospitals.

Use government's exclusive position to investigate and monitor the hospitals and administration to ensure the quality of care is high and the money is being spent properly.

The care at the charity hospitals won't match the private hospitals, but healthcare won't be 'equal' when the government takes over either. Those with the means will always be able to pay for the best.

Making it impossible for those in the middle to have a choice in healthcare planning and options so that we can all be 'equal' is not an improvement, it's just spreading misery for the sake of securing power for bureaucrats and politicians.

Equality of outcome is not fairness, it's not justice. It's just a new way of saying that winners and losers will be chosen in advance, not determined based on merit.

Equality of opportunity is what we should focus on, and as our nation has forgotten the difference between the two, the result has been the creation of a system that manages to make objective fairness and justice far less likely to occur in our daily lives.

Culture War, What is it Good For?

Before we get to the discussion of how to turn back the tide - and make no mistake, it will be a monumental task - we will need to take a step back and realize our limitations.

We - those of us who are tired of being pawns in someone else's chess game - must resist the temptation to allow the use of government power for social ends we support, especially because the temptation power breeds is the achilles heel of people who otherwise believe in limited government.

The rallying cry of those favoring expanded government benefits, services, and entitlements has been, in every election that I can remember, the specter of 'social conservatives' and 'evangelicals' creating a joyless theocracy.

If you listen to those speaking for the young, hip, cool, urban, sophisticated, libertine, etc., letting the conservatives win is the next worst thing to bringing back the Spanish Inquisition.

Even though nobody is expecting it, the thought still manages to get all the young and morally flexible to cast their vote leftward to avoid having a bunch of prudes put limits on their fun.

Of course, it wasn't conservatives who have outlawed cigarettes, foie gras, trans fats, tried to outlaw salt, and have decided to fix the epidemic of fat kids by increasing access to school lunches - which studies have shown is a major factor in childhood obesity.

But conservatives as a whole - and if you aren't on board with growing government control, you are considered 'conservative' - have a reputation for being... busybody prigs quick to use the law to punish immorality.

Use of recreational intoxicants?   Conservatives call for expanding the drug war, and publicly blame the media and entertainment industry for making drug use seem cool and acceptable, and basically play the dorky high school busybody role in real life.

Pornography exploding online? Conservatives demand restrictions on the spread of filth and clamor for the government to do something about this plague of obscenity, and the most public voices often end up on the wrong side of scandal.

Anything related to rap music, raunchy entertainment, or general immorality? Conservatives leaders and politicians are in front of the mob, leading the calls for greater restrictions on these threats to the fabric of our society.

The fact is, the history of conservative leadership is filled with very public moments of being really, really judgmental, annoying, intolerant, intrusive, hypocritical, condescending, preachy... yeah, that's good enough for now.

Rarely do these leaders fail seize an opportunity to reinforce that image by supporting new laws to restrict 'immoral' actions.

Mitch Daniels, governor of Indiana - an amazingly tolerant, boring, and industrious state I've had the pleasure of spending time working in - had a roundabout moment of clarity on this weakness when he suggested that conservatives call a truce on social issues and focus on the basics of liberty and economics.

Naturally, this was heard as a betrayal of the highest order by the social conservative groups that depend on outrageously outraged people to donate money and support their mission to make this country conform to their view of the righteous path of... righteousness.

This presents a real problem to those of us who see the threat of a society with no moral backbone, yet have a deep fear of men like Mike Huckabee eventually preaching from the Oval Office.

Speaking the Gospel to guide your flock is one thing, but using Biblical text to sell tax increases or restrict liberty is another.

If only there was a way to solve this problem while understanding that government has it's limits. Hmmm....

One solution - simple, elegant, and really hard for some people to swallow - lies in the following statement:

You can't legislate morality.

It's a tough one to get down, I know. But the more you try to control a population through government intervention, the more you entice people to find out what is on the other side.

Worse still, the more you try to use the law to enforce your version of morality, the more your ideological enemies will use the same powers you create to enforce their version of morality.

If we are ever going to achieve less government in our lives, we have to accept the fact that if we choose to let government control the lives of others, the more we open the door to control over ourselves.

This is why the battle between the Republicans and Democrats has become a decision between who will control your lives, not whether we will allow others to have control.

The Tea Parties are so attractive to independents because they don't play by the same special interest rules, and are focused on fiscal responsibility and limited government.

Don't get me wrong - this is not a call for anarchy, Amsterdam-esque openness to anything and everything, or endorsement of the latest perversion of our youth.

It's a plea to stop trying to solve every problem using government - even the social problems you and your allies care deeply about.

The way to combat erosion of morality isn't through the government, it's through the individual. Using the power of the state to enforce one idea of what is right v. another merely serves to drive communities apart.

It's a losing proposition for all sides as the morally-righteous/politically-naive and the liberty minded iconoclasts go to war and the politicians use that friction to increase their power.

It doesn't have to be that way, but it will take some very serious, very real commitment to the idea that we can't pass laws to make people better.

We need to stop thinking that the government will solve our problems or that making various actions, intoxicants, or ideas illegal will eradicate them from the populace.

It has never worked, and it never will. Instead of proposing a new law or program with every time some new plague strikes, give back the tools for people to address the problems themselves.

As citizens, we need to get on the ball and start taking responsibility for the past decline and, hopefully, the rebirth of our nation as the greatest on Earth.

Part of that process is understanding that we cannot allow government to take responsibility for what we can only accomplish ourselves.

We need to teach our children, our friends, and ourselves that the road to health, wealth, and happiness runs not through the path of cheap thrills and immediate gratification, but through a life of honesty, dignity, and integrity.

Taking back responsibility will be a process, not an event, and should focus on some specific changes to our own role in society.

Get involved in local meetings and events, build some neighborly bonds that can handle stress, encourage people to call out for help when they need it and stop being afraid to point out when someone is on a path of destruction.

The time and effort necessary to create a community is daunting, and opposition among the same busybodies who have created housing projects, midnight basketball, and methadone clinics is sure to be fierce.

But would it be a bad thing if we had a return to the type of public involvement and community outreach that handled problems at the local level?

If the problem escalated to the point that the police needed to be involved - when you have threats of violence, the rise of gang activity, etc. - the police would be working with a strong community, not against them as infiltrators and agitators.

It's not an easy battle, and there will be lives lost to the temptation of drugs, alcohol, weird and exotic pleasures - all the stuff that has tempted mankind since man and woman put on the leaf.

But those lives lost are the same ones that are lost today in communities where the dealers and the addicts get free food, free rent, and neighborhoods are ruled by gangs and fear the police as much or more than the junkie.

Over the last 4 decades, we've seen the alternative in action, removing moral and religious education from the classroom, attempting to legislate a more moral populace through regulation, increasing legal consequences while protecting people from the scorn and influence of their neighbors, and taking responsibility away from the people and putting it in the hands of government.

We have tried to understand and nurture people away from drug abuse, teaching them that what they do is wrong but not too feel too bad about it - it's a disease, not your fault, feel no shame.

We've seen the commercials, the public service announcements, and the government campaigns - from Just Say No to 'If you get high, the terrorists will use that money to mutilate babies. And puppies. Puppies'.

Those campaigns have been just as effective as most other programs, so effective in fact that there isn't a drug dealer in America that doesn't have a D.A.R.E. sticker somewhere in his possession.

Understand, I'm not advocating the end of drug abuse education. But we need to get more than just the technical information and propaganda in front of the children. A local approach that involves the community and gives a real picture of the drug experience would be far more effective.

Try this: 'You'll feel funny and laugh for a few hours. The next day you'll either feel like shit or just plain stupid, and if you do enough drugs you'll forget to shower, flunk out of school, and eventually end up in rehab, live in a cardboard box, or die in a slum. Here are pictures of people who did a lot of drugs, then and now.'

Sounds a lot scarier and realistic than the classic propaganda films people watch while high to this day, don't you think?

We also need to better prepare our children for the pressures of life by giving them a better foundation from the start, getting in front of the issues early by demanding a return to educating children about values.

It would have to start early, with the re-introduction of teaching ethics, and removing obstacles - financial and legal - to the mention of religious principles in public schools or attendance at parochial schools in the cities.

The removal of the concept of morality from schools in a misguided attempt to separate church and state has done real damage to our society.

It's past time to do for our public school educated children what the wealthy and the pious do for theirs - give them a historical, values-based moral education to build their lives upon.

Next, we need to accept that the only way to build a better society is to educate those will listen, help those who seek it, and take the advice of Frederick Douglass:

If the apples will not remain on the tree of their own strength, if they are wormeaten at the core, if they are early ripe and disposed to fall, let them fall!

It's a hard choice to make, especially the closer the person falling is to you. You look for people to blame and ways to make sure nobody has to feel the same pain.

But we have to make the choice to deal with it ourselves or accept that our compassion will be used against us. Allowing politicians to turn everything into a moral issue that requires their intervention only serves politicians as the rest of us pay the price for relinquishing control.

Take back responsibility for our own families and neighborhoods. Understand that a better society can only come about at the individual level.

Reliance on law as a substitute for a values will always fail. You can't legislate morality simply because it has not, will not, and will never work.

If you have a compulsion driving you to make the larger world a better place, volunteer to speak to children, start a foundation, a charity, a support group - these things will make a difference in the lives of others as well as your own.

If you feel the need to restrict the liberties of others to ensure they never have the opportunity to make the same mistake as you, the one you lost, or some distant group of nameless, faceless toiling masses - step back and rethink your plans.

All you will create is a beast that will just as soon swallow you as those you wish to control, and the sacrifice in liberty will be devastating for us all.

We Don't Need No Reeducation

I touched a bit on education, but the topic requires a closer look.

One of the most troubling ways that people seeking greater power have abused the public trust is by changing the style, nature, and focus of public education system.

This is one of a number of areas where government intervention and some type of standards are necessary, but the decisions they make have to be monitored and scrutinized heavily.

Under the guidance of teacher's unions and the Department of Education, the focus of our schools has shifted dramatically. Once, schools focused on preparing children to leave their mandatory education with the right set of skills to function in society.

The growth of the home schooling movement, the continued existence of private schooling and the battle over school voucher programs are a direct result of the continuing failure of public schooling to provide what was advertised: prepare the nation's children for life as an adult.

Now, while I'm not opposed to the options of home schooling, private schooling, or private/parochial school vouchers - allowing families to choose the best option for their children is a necessary way to gauge what is working and what isn't - I do think we need to take a hard look at public education and figure out how to fix the glaring problems that exist.

First and foremost, we need to focus on the curriculum.

Reading, writing, and arithmetic absolutely must be the center of the educational system - if you can't read for yourself, express yourself clearly, or perform the basic calculations of everyday life, you will not be able to take advantage of the opportunities being an American provides.

I would think this was self evident, but since nearly half of all incoming college freshmen require remedial education just to get up to speed, this clearly needs more attention.*

Next, basic history, literature, civics, economics, science and technology should be the next step once a proven proficiency in the first three areas has been established. The focus of the additional subjects should include reference and solidification of the original big 3 topics.

A curriculum like that - which insists on proficiency in each subject before moving on to another or graduating - would be a great way to prepare every high school graduate to get a basic job or move on to college.

It would also give kids some skills to use in the real world, a novel concept when we now consider 26 year olds to be 'children', but maybe turning out some adults at 18 would help to turn that around as well.

Of course, the outline I've put out there may seem familiar, mainly because it is nominally the standard curriculum of public schools we all remember from our youth. But we still have failing schools.

Solving this problem will take real action by individuals, parents, and families that go beyond signing report cards and making sure they do their homework.

We need to reintroduce the freedom for children to fail, and accept the fact that their failure is a sign of parental failure as well.

They need to understand that there are consequences for the choices they make, and their parents need to accept their role in producing a functioning, successful adult.

Parents also need to stop attacking teachers who diagnose the failing youth and start holding the kids to higher standards.

For those people concerned about the self esteem of kids who have to repeat grades until they get them right, think about how much more humiliating it is to be the kid who can't read, write, or solve a basic math problem. For the rest of their lives.

The subjects themselves will require modification and parental vigilance as well. Twenty years ago I underwent biology class taught by a middle aged hippy who used every day as her little ecological soapbox.

I didn't learn much about mitochondria, photosynthesis, or whatever else is normally taught in biology course, but I can still visualize the graphs showing the dangers of CFCs and DDT.

Neither of which was of much use as I struggled to catch up with the class during my college science requirement.

Children need to be taught the basics of becoming a functioning adult, including some religious concepts and values, and leave the nuanced theories, political controversies, indoctrination, and experimental ideas to the kids who have the curiosity and desire to continue their education into college.

Introducing concepts and classes in high school or younger that revolve around hyphenated '-justice' or '-studies' in particular (social-justice, environmental-justice,   racial justice, ethnic studies, women's studies, environmental justice, etc.) are doing more harm than good.

They only serve a purpose for academics, activists, and ideologues, and should be left for a child's university rebellion phase - and even there should be discussed in coordination with competing principles instead of preached as gospel.

Taking millions of children every year and giving them a one-sided view of ideas that require time and energy to understand completely only serves to advance the interest of people who understand that like fire, a 'little knowledge' is both a dangerous and a useful thing if you can control it.

But that's not the only reason to be against introducing divisive ideas that are only useful as term paper thesis and political polemics.

When these kids get into the real world, the majority find themselves unable to understand the very basic realities of economics and business because they've been taught that both of those things are merely tools used to inflict all variety of 'injustice'.

This is a failing that has far reaching consequences, with these kids having to overcome deeply ingrained prejudices against the people they will likely be working for.

They also have to unlearn all they were taught about the evils of capitalism in order to understand concepts like supply and demand, opportunity costs, the law of diminishing returns, and that treating the person who gives you a job like an enemy is a surefire way to gain an enemy and lose a job.

In the major metropolitan areas, where the problems faced in the schools are far more severe than in the suburban or rural districts, some other, more drastic measures are called for.

The following idea - shared with me by a group of teachers in the South Bronx, NY - is one that you will never hear from the leaders of their union, but were widely praised by this mixed group that included a number of races, ages, genders and positions at their school, and is related as true to life as I can recall:

In any standard public school population, you have basically three groups - the ones who want to succeed, the ones who want to get by, and the ones who are only going to cause trouble.   The percentage in each group will vary, but the grouping remains essentially the same.

For the kids who are in the ambitious and successful segment, you offer either a voucher to a private or parochial school or an advanced education campus - and you allow their parents to choose which, not the district.

This will give the kids who are naturally high-achieving the type of environment that will challenge them and give them an opportunity to take advantage of their abilities and ambitions.

For the kids who are there to cause trouble, they need to be removed to facilities specifically designed to keep them from the other kids. These kids are not hard to spot, and need to be removed early to keep them from hurting themselves and others. It's also an early lesson that bad behavior will lead to separation from society.

Give these kids the opportunity to test back into regular schools every year and prove that they can change, but stop spending so much time worrying about the world they come from and put some focus on the world they are creating for their classmates.

The kids in the middle? Well, they are the ones who right now get lost between the high achievers and the delinquents. They don't need advanced concepts and political spin, they need skills. They don't need to worry about bullies and gang-bangers, they need teachers that can answer questions and explain the work - not spend half the class arguing with kids passing time before heading to Rikers Island.

Again, these aren't old concepts, and this was not my idea. Teachers see the need. School districts used to do exactly this with the kids, and it worked well, if not perfect. It's a return to old wisdom instead of changing standards and methods for the sake of change itself.

The fact is, we used to understand that teaching usable skills and basic ethics would create a better citizen than self esteem workshops, political indoctrination, and abandonment of standards. Most of us still get it.

But teacher's union leaders, politicians, and activists have spent the last few decades dismantling a traditional understanding that all kids are not the same.

Because we allowed education to become run without our input, and then accepted that we needed a federal bureaucracy to take responsibility for the process, we lost control of what our children learned.

The only way we are going to take back the schools and change the future of our children is for citizens and parents to get involved.

Dismantle the institutions that control the educational content, and take responsibility for the next generation ourselves instead of ceding control to people who do not have the children's best interest in mind - they have their own ambitions to fulfill and ideas to spread.

*USA Today, 9/28/05, Colleges spend billions on remedial classes to prep freshmen (http://www.usatoday.com/news/education/2008-09-15-Colleges-remedialclasses_N.htm)

Your Mission, Should You Choose to Run for Office

As I said earlier, I'm not some anarchist that wants to see government destroyed. I do see a need for an overarching institution that performs specific functions - the heart of which being the protection of the rights of the smallest minority, the individual.

This is what the founders fought and died for, and it is important we elect leaders who not only understand their role, but perform their part with the most transparency possible.

This entails many small but important changes, the first of which should be writing laws that are understandable without a lawyer. You do this action, which hurts these people, and you will be punished with a fine, jail time, etc.

Regulations also need to be written so that any business, big or small, can understand the rules they need to follow to stay out of trouble. The regulations we have in place today require legal action just to figure out the boundaries the bureaucracies put in place.

This is, excuse the expression, a crap sandwich we are consistently asked to swallow, which coincidentally gives a massive advantage to larger corporations with teams of lawyers on staff to translate and lobby to guide the eventual scope of the law.

In that same vein, government needs to go back and revisit, revise, and repeal a whole mess of laws and regulations on the books that violate the basic protection of the individual's right to make his own decisions and responsibility to deal with the consequences.

Protection of rights does not include paying for constituent food and housing, making sure earmarks and projects are directed towards donors, or creating new bureaucracies that increase the number of people feeding off other people's taxes.

The embrace of an individual rights focused government will hopefully lead to judges realizing that their role is not to make new policy, create new rights, or right perceived wrongs.

The job of the judicial branch of government is to make sure law is administered blindly, and that each law that is challenged in their courtrooms falls within the powers given to the government by the Constitution.

If it doesn't, then the law is unjust. If it does - and the law was written in a way that the intent and violation of that law is clearly defined - then the law stands.

Simplifying the laws of the land may mean less work for the courts, but I'm OK with getting some of those brilliant minds in Washington back into the real world, doing something actually useful with their time.

Which is a great segue to another important point!

I'm not going to deny that the people who go to Washington, state capitals, county seats or city hall are bright people with a great deal of ambition, energy, and drive to do great things. The people who make it into positions of leadership tend be high achieving, driven, and quite bright, all things considered.

But there are way to many of these bright minds dedicated to grabbing for the reigns of power to drive the nation in the direction of their needs. In the end, as Twain said, they all go to Washington to do good, and stay to do well.

I'm supremely confident that if these people could come up with some amazing innovations and improvements in the lives of others if only they would stop trying to use government to implement their dreams, gain some real-world experience, and create something that gives people better choices rather than try to force change upon us.

Young minds in Washington, I beg of you - take some of that brilliance and dedication to ideas and use it to build a better... anything. That is the only proven, long term way to make a real difference. in the lives of the citizens of this nation and any other.

Thomas Sowell, the Hoover Institution economist, actually did an analysis and showed that if you really want to have a positive impact on society, the most effective way to do so isn't through activism or legislation, but by starting a business.

Starting a company not only creates jobs and wealth, but gives people the experience and skills to one day step out and create their own business, continuing the cycle.

Those who do feel the urge to serve the nation from the perch of government should be focused on making sure that the government is working for the people and not the other way around.

The debates on taxation are so focused on funding ever expanding programs that the fact that taxation is essentially legislated theft is lost in the wash. We need leaders who understand that growing government revenue is actually a bad thing, not a sign of progress.

The other thing that government should focus on is making sure that people aren't being illegally abused or hurt by others - especially those in government.

This is the essence of equal protection, and sadly, those in governance have been so focused on getting reelected, they seem to have forgotten that simple mission. This has generated some very troubling examples of how the power of government is being abused and misdirected.

Wall Street donors in trouble? Bail them out!

Unions in danger of driving their company into bankruptcy? Time to nationalize and give the company to the unions!

Activist group demands new regulations to save the desert milkweed? Protect that weed by any means necessary!

In all of the cases above, resources were taken from average citizens for the sake of the connected and protected. In all of them - and many others - the government isn't righting a wrong, they are actually harming individuals for the sake of their allies. This is the opposite of what government should do.

Stocks tacking a tumble? Follow Andrew Mellon's advice and liquidate, liquidate, liquidate - the market will clean out the trash itself.

Union pensions and work rules destroying GM and Chrysler? Allow the companies to go under and other companies will buy the assets and rebuild with the knowledge that the old ways were unsustainable.

A weed in the sand dunes of California in danger from recreational dirt bike riders? Let the sand weed go the way of the dodo, nobody will miss it.

If those points didn't get through, office seekers and holders, please, for all that is good and holy, remember that when you asked for permission to represent us, the basis of that permission was the protection of our rights and interests.

Hold true to that standard, and stop raiding the Treasury and our liberties to keep your seats.

D-E-F-E-N-S-E, Find Out What It Means To Me

There is one area where government is the only viable, vital institution in the lives of the citizens - defense. I've got a number of reasons why I will nearly always err spending too much on defense.

Because we live in a world where evil still exists;

Because there are nations that harbor the same ambitions that have always driven men to conquer both neighboring and far away lands;

Because there are people who believe in killing of those who do not worship the same God as they do, or do it in a different way;

Because there are leaders whose lust for money and power will drive them to do unspeakable things to anyone who stands in their way.

These are some of the reasons why we need to defend the seas, the shores, the land, and the principles our nation was founded upon.

The only way to effectively defend our nation is with a national defense force . No matter who you are or what you believe, it is the military that protects us all from threats abroad.

A government based military is the only entity that can effectively defend our nation from foreign threats, and needs to do so on the border, the high seas, in the skies, etc. because unlike a private military, it isn't for sale to the highest bidder. It fights for the nation, not for the money.

You can argue about how it should be used, where it should be based, what it should spend money to build - and we should argue about these things.

But the need to protect the nation from foreign threats is very real, and needs to be taken more seriously.

Especially on the border, because that is where our laws and principles end and, frankly, a much more savage world begins.

I mean, we know Canada pretty well, but do we really know Canada? Long dark winters can take a toll on the mind. I'm just sayin' is all.

Additionally, the members and veterans of the military are, in my opinion, the sole exception to my anti-entitlement beliefs. Mainly because unlike most entitlements, these were earned through service.

We should treat those who volunteer to serve in the military as the only legitimate recipients of government benefits.

The current healthcare battle largely ignores the fact that our VA hospital system needs some serious overhaul.

If the government wants to work on healthcare, work on the VA - make it work so well that people line up to join the military and earn the right to free healthcare for life.

Anyone who tries to argue that we need to dramatically scale back on our military men and equipment; that we should be spending our defense money on handouts and entitlements; or that we don't actually need a military is an idiot or an enemy of the nation.

And that's about all I have to say about that.

The Rest

There are other areas where government is vital to keeping the nation moving forward. When looking for these areas, know that there should be a common thread among them - they offer the same opportunity and benefit to everyone.

Easiest to pick out is infrastructure. Roads, bridges, tunnels, water lines, electrical grids - as the richest nation on earth, we should have the best of all these things, and having travelled abroad, I can confidently say that we almost do.

Then again, I've worked all five boroughs of New York, Boston, Chicago, Detroit, Los Angeles - all the places where a whole lot of money is spent to support people who don't work, and the infrastructure in the less opulent parts of town is nearly always in serious need of repair - or in the case of Vermont, dirt roads are common.

Here's an idea - use the money currently slotted for social services and hire people who need work to pave the roads, repair the sidewalks, replace aging utilities - and end the laws that require all union labor to do federal, state, and municipal work.

Using these funds to create a skilled workforce - instead of serving as full employment schemes for bureaucrats and union leaders - will do a lot to build better cities and provide opportunities instead of entitlements.

It will also keep people off the streets and idle hands busy. If we can do it without wasting millions on propaganda signs to promote trillion dollar slush funds, all the better.

Which brings me to a quick side note: Its funny how often old principles and wisdom keep popping up, especially when a new generation of arrogant young leaders decides they know better than a few thousand years of developed wisdom.

There are other areas of mutual protection requiring government attention.

Pollution is a mutual problem, and as much as I hate the EPA's efforts to regulate everything from carbon to bullets, the fact is we need to have a government agency in charge of enforcing the laws against polluting our air and water.

But instead of giving the agency carte blanche regulatory authority with oversight that is more political than constitutional, the EPA needs to be investigating and enforcing laws, not determining what is and is not a pollutant or what constitutes a violation of the regulations created with no means of realistic appeal.

Leave the determination of what is a crime or violation to the lawmakers in Congress. Unlike the EPA, when Congress reaches to far and starts making silly and/or damaging rules, we have an opportunity to fire them.

Apply this same standard throughout the government - leave the regulation and lawmaking to the elected leaders and reserve any bureaucracy left over to handle enforcement - and we can cut back on a lot of wasted money, effort, and get a handle on problems that we all see.

But even with these changes, we have to remain involved, because the 'mutual protection' standard is a good starting point, but it has weaknesses.

Elected officials and tyrants alike call for 'helping those in need' as part of their platforms, which nearly always precedes leadership in transition from representative to ruling, spinning their efforts to control our lives as expressions of compassion and charity.

The way we stop the unscrupulous and power hungry from taking us down that road is by using the one power that is given to the average citizen, the passengers in this great nation - the power to choose who will be given the privilege of protecting our rights.

The relationship between the lawmakers and the citizens, where overreach leads to dismissal, is one that we need to maintain if we are to keep our power in this republic. In order to do that, we need to keep interested, informed, and involved in our local, state, and federal governments.

We need to keep those who ask for the privilege to represent us focused on the tasks government is uniquely qualified to manage, steering the nation forward and keeping us out of the rocks - and leave the rest alone.

We need to remember that we are better suited to control our own lives and deal with our own failures and those of our communities; and that we will create a better bond among the people when we help each other voluntarily and learn to be grateful for the generosity of our fellow citizens.

If we can learn to live in a society built on individual rights, responsibilities, and mutual respect the nation won't be perfect, but it will move in a far better direction.

If we cannot, then we will devolve into exactly what our forefathers fought to free themselves - and by extension all of us - from living under.

The author in front of Congress, 2003. Note the stoplights are on red, a happy accident.

Also note that author does not always smile like that, he just has a bad habit of acting up in pictures, and as such there are many photos of him looking like this, sticking out his tongue, glaring like a madman, or looking like he smells something rotten in Denmark.

The author's family and friends shouldn't share those pictures.

Ever.